Anonym

Leveraged Buyouts (LBO) in private equity deals

Deal structure, risk structure and governance implications in LBO transactions

GRIN Verlag

Bibliografische Information der Deutschen Nationalbibliothek:

Die Deutsche Bibliothek verzeichnet diese Publikation in der Deutschen National-
bibliografie; detaillierte bibliografische Daten sind im Internet über http://dnb.d-
nb.de/ abrufbar.

Imprint:

Copyright © 2007 GRIN Verlag GmbH
Druck und Bindung: Books on Demand GmbH, Norderstedt Germany
ISBN: 978-3-640-20454-0

This book at GRIN:

http://www.grin.com/en/e-book/90175/leveraged-buyouts-lbo-in-private-equity-
deals

GRIN - Your knowledge has value

Der GRIN Verlag publiziert seit 1998 wissenschaftliche Arbeiten von Studenten, Hochschullehrern und anderen Akademikern als eBook und gedrucktes Buch. Die Verlagswebsite www.grin.com ist die ideale Plattform zur Veröffentlichung von Hausarbeiten, Abschlussarbeiten, wissenschaftlichen Aufsätzen, Dissertationen und Fachbüchern.

Visit us on the internet:

http://www.grin.com/

http://www.facebook.com/grincom

http://www.twitter.com/grin_com

EUROPEAN BUSINESS SCHOOL

International University Schloss Reichartshausen

Seminar Paper

Seminar in Corporate Finance

Fall Term 2007

Leveraged Financing of Private Equity Deals

-

Deal Structure, Risk Structure and Governance Implications

Subject: Corporate Finance

Submission Date: November 12, 2007

Table of Contents

1   Executive Summary

Igniting in 2005, the discussion about highly leveraged transactions conducted by financial institutions became a matter of great controversy in German politics as well as in the media. Fuelled by an influential voice in politics, LBO firms became the face of capitalism's evil by calling them a "Heuschrecke", an animal much feared in history for its exploitive behaviour and risks to the mediaeval agrarian economy (Die Zeit, 2005). In terms of today's Heuschrecke, according to public voice, downsizing and raiding represent the major risks attributed.

Empirics show that the risk of downsizing in LBOs is falsified and that the occurrence of raids is rather irrelevant in today's buyout universe. However, even if both risks held, each would exhibit a comparably low impact on the economy as a whole.

Contrary, the empirically evident high-impact risk of over-indebtedness in leveraged transactions is widely neglected. The negligence of this risk-issue is dangerous, particularly with regard to the recent developments in the LBO industry, debt capital markets and the world's economy. First, analysing the latest LBOs conducted, it appears that the historical failures, such as the buyouts of Revco and RJR Narbisco are widely forgotten, as gearing ratios have become aggressive again. Second, the subprime crisis, which was exported from the US real estate sector into global capital markets, caused liquidity shortages – AA rated banks were not willing to lend money to their equally rated peers anymore – which led to a credit crisis. This credit crunch provoked that, even though in the US the prime rate has been reduced by 50 bp, and in the Eurozone the prime rate was not increased as planed, 'money became expensive'; FIBOR, LIBOR and EURIBOR sharply increased and remained high. This resulted in high debt funding costs. Third, taking a look at the world economy, America might face an economic downturn in the near future with decreasing consumption and increasing inflation. Furthermore, political tensions e.g. between the United States and Iran can quickly lead to an increase in commodity prices.

Each of the three aspects alone increases the default risk in a highly leveraged firm. In a scenario where all three jointly appear, the probability of default will sharply increase.

To draw a worst case scenario:

The American economy runs into recession. Owing to strong global interdependency's in trade, the US recession causes a worldwide economic downturn. Diverse states further lower their prime rate to counteract, inflation rises, however inter-bank-offer rates remain unaffected. As a consequence, LBO transactions will increasingly run into default. This will further worsen the economic climate. After several defaults, the LBO fim's will be unable to hide "the walking wounded", thus, investors in LBO funds will want to rescue their money. An "LBO fund run" starts. However, LBOs are illiquid investments, particularly in a economic downturn as secondary buyouts and IPO activity will converge to zero.

In addition to the risk named, the threat an LBO imposes on global debt capital markets is evident, therefore, it can not be ignored any longer in Europe. While it was already heavily discussed in America's late 80s and early 90s buyout-boom, it slowly gains prominence in discussions LBO transactions.

1.1 Course of Investigation

In the face of the concrete course of the investigation, the first three chapters will shed light on the buyout itself and will discuss critical issues in the deal's structure. The components described in the section are chosen with regard to their high importance for the success of the deal and the risks involved. The fourth chapter mainly discusses the risks encountered by investors, companies and the financial system with regard to LBO transactions. Finally, the last part of the paper deals with governance implications in LBO transactions. In particular, the quest for stronger regulations is investigated and the practical relevance of Jensen's free cash flow hypothesis is evaluated.

1.2 Definition of an LBO

Analysing recent buyouts, a broad band of deals can be observed. While in some deals a public company is taken private, in others a privately held company is subjected to acquisition. However, all buyouts observed feature three main attributes, namely high gearing[1], constrained lenders' claims[2] and high return on the equity invested[3].

Therefore, for the purpose of this paper, buyout is defined as "an undertaking by private investors, including a buyout fund, members of the management team and sometimes

---

[1] Cf. Brealey & Myers, 2005, p. 1067; Pohlhausen, 2003, p. 6.
2 Cf. Machiraju, 2003, p. 180; Pohlhausen, 2003, p. 6.
[3] The statement "high" is in accordance with literature that specifies 30 to 40% return on equity in LBOs which is higher than the returns on the S&P 500. "During the 1990s, for instance, venture capital (here: venture capital covers both buyouts and seed finance) funds earned an average return of 29.5%, compared to the S&P 500's annual return of 15.1%" (Damodaran, 2003, p. 308). In accordance with Loos (2006, p.14), "LBO firms generally target a 25-35% IRR in buyout executions." Cf. Machiraju, 2003, p. 180; Brealey & Myers, 2005, p. 1067; KKR, 1989, p. 4.

also employees, to acquire a company or the subsidiary of a company through a large amount of debt capital, secured by the target company's assets, and a small amount of equity" (Meier, 2006, pp. 14-15; Wright, Robbie, Thomson & Starkey, 1993, pp. 30, 216; Achleitner & Fingerle, 2003, p. 3; Easterwood, Seth & Singer, 1989, p. 30).

2   How Does an LBO Work

In an LBO – besides other levers – equity is created through the use of debt and the advantages debt features over equity. These advantages, namely cheaper funding and tax deductibility, assure that by using the firm's free cash flow to pay off a high debt facility, value is created. Furthermore, this means that neither organic growth nor operational changes need to be conducted in order to achieve high equity returns (Baker & Smith, 2006, p. 60). From a very basic perspective, two key issues are necessary to conduct an LBO on an appropriate target, namely high gearing and sufficient cash flow. With regard to the first, although no perfect debt to equity ratio exists, yet return on equity but also risk is maximised when the target's financial structure is composed of 10 to 20% equity and 80 to 90% debt and the amortization period is about five years (Baker & Smith, 2006, p. 60). In terms of the second, constantly high cash flows are vital for success; thus the target's respective management must refocus from revenue creation to cash flow creation. Applying the two key issues, the following transaction represents a first example:[4]

A 100% equity financed pencil manufacturer constantly produces a cash flow of $20m. After market screening, due diligence, valuation and strategy development, the deal is signed and closed. As financial structure for the firm and for the payment of the transaction amount to $100m, the LBO firm contributes $30m equity and $70m in debt. After the acquisition, the LBO firm advises the acquired firm's management to strictly focus on the generation of cash flow. This strict focus leads to improved operations, superior asset utilisation as well as more efficient capital investments which increase the firm's free cash flow to slightly over $26m. Furthermore, it is decided that the cash flow is primarily used to pay off the $70m debt facility since the tax shield can be fully used by following this strategy. Since it is a highly leveraged transaction, it is furthermore assumed that the average interest on debt is prime rate plus a 500 bp spread, leading to

---

[4] General idea derived in accordance with Baker & Smith, 2006, p. 60; Data: Own model Appendix, Scenario 1.

an interest rate of 10% per annum. Calculating the debt service on the data provided, the target will have paid off the entire facility within five years.

Assuming that the firm is sold for the former purchase price, $100m, at exit point the former $30m equity stake is worth $100m. The LBO fund receives a capital gain of $70m solely through a strict cash flow focus and the use of high gearing.

3   Deal Structure

A leveraged buyout is composed of four major sequent components. The process is initiated by the deal flow and screening phase. Less than 30% of the former screened potential targets become analysed more detailed in the due diligence and acquisition phase (Gröne, 2005, pp. 14-15). The due diligence and acquisition phase is terminated by either a 'no-go' or the signing and closing of the acquisition. After a successful closing, the monitoring and advising phase – which last for 3 to 7 years – commences and ends when a carefully planed exit is executed.

3.1   Deal Flow and Screening Phase

Although a buyout fund contributes major key factors to the transaction, such as excellent funding abilities, extensive networks, market knowledge and experience, not every firm represents an ideal target for a leveraged buyout. In order to find out which firms represent targets, "the buyout process begins with a 'target selection' phase, in which the LBO firm screens the market for investment opportunities meeting the rigid criteria for a successful LBO candidate" (Loos, 2006, p. 14). These can be classified as financial and business criteria (Loos, 2006, pp. 12-14; Gröne, 2005, pp.12-13).

3.1.1   Financial Criteria

Financial criteria play the key role in deciding whether an LBO can be conducted on the target or not, since it evaluates the credit worthiness of the target's business. In this evaluation, strong, stable and predictable cash flows are the most crucial issue because the target must be able to cope with high gearing (Graebner, 1991, p. 19). Second, the potential target must possess non-core assets which can be sold in order to quickly obtain liquidity (Loos, 2006, p.13). These non-core assets serve as a safety net since the high financing cost caused by extensive gearing must be paid regardless the operational success of the business. As a third aspect, "a history of demonstrated profitability and the ability to maintain above average profit margins" is essential (Loos, 2006, p. 13;

KKR, 1989, pp. 2-5). This is fact, since profit margins are closely related to free cash flow and thus essential. Furthermore, profit margins must be high since changes in the industry can lower the margins at any given point in time.

With regard to financial criteria, each is based on assumptions, estimated predictions and historical data; stable cash flows can change in the future, there might be no potential buyer for the non-core assets, and high profit margins may have been fact solely in the past.

3.1.2 Business Criteria

Besides financial criteria, business criteria are the second layer that needs to be assed before a transaction is conducted. With regard to these criteria, it is essential that the target feature's a well-known brand name as well as a strong market position. This is crucial since both contribute to the stability of cash flow generation, play a key role when selling the firm at the exit and feature downside protection in terms of competition. Second, it is essential that the target operates in a non-cyclical industry particularly regarding the recent economic development since the risk of cash flow shortage 'in the wrong moment' must be avoided. Third, the target's technology mix must be stable and not subject to rapid technological change. Fourth, the target must have a realistic and viable business plan as well as a competitive advantage (Loos, 2006, p. 13).

3.2   Due Diligence and Acquisition Phase

After the target has been selected, a due diligence is performed, the terms of the transaction are negotiated, the holding structure is developed, plans and contracts with the current or potential management are made, and a detailed financial package to pay for the acquisition is developed.

3.2.1 Due Diligence

The due diligence is performed in order the gather all necessary information related to the target in order to make an appropriate offer. A due diligence consists of three major components, namely the basic due diligence, the external due diligence and the strategic due diligence (Picot, 2005, p. 295). In the basic due diligence all publicly available data about the firm is gathered and analysed (Picot, 2005, pp. 295-296). The external due diligence focuses on the analyses of economic issues related to the firm as well as the markets the firm is operating in. The strategic due diligence can be subdivided into marketing due diligence, human resource due diligence, legal and tax due diligence, environmental due diligence and financial due diligence. With regard to the components, the financial due diligence and the marketing due diligence represent the major issues with regard to an LBO.

The financial due diligence aims at analysing the balance sheets, profit and loss accounts, cash flow statements, and all other internal, financial data relevant for the acquisition (Picot, 2005, p. 298). Hence, it analyses if the target features all relevant financial criteria.

The marketing due diligence is closely liked to the financial due diligence, it focuses on the chances and risk associated with the target itself and the target's market (Picot, 2005, p. 301). Thus, is serves as tool to evaluate upon the target's business criteria.

3.2.2   Acquisition Structure

The acquisition of a target can be conducted as asset deal or as share deal. In a share deal, the legal entity, with all its "liabilities, including contingent and unknown liabilities become the responsibility of the buyer" (Michel & Sharked, 1988, p. 256; Picot, 2005, p. 139). Contrary, in an asset deal only specifically named and valued assets of the target are bought while legal agreements, such as contacts, are excluded; they can only be included if renegotiated by the respective parties involved (Michel & Sharked, 1988, p. 249; Picot, 2005, p. 141).

Comparing the two acquisition structures, each features advantages and drawbacks, yet "there is no 'best' structure for all leveraged buyouts" (Michel and Shaked, 1988, p. 247). While an asset deal needs exact specification and thus consumes time, a share deal is performed comparably fast. However, since an asset deal demands precise specification, it is the safer transaction for the fund because it assures that no claims are overlooked which would obligate the fund in a share deal.

3.2.3 Holding Structure

Analysing the general concept of LBO transactions, diverse and strongly varying holding structures need to be evaluated in each respective context. Since each transaction is unique, the parties' interests and the financial structure determine which structure will be applied. However, the most crucial element of each structure is that the interest costs for the debt facility must be entirely tax deductible, thus, the structure is always mainly tax driven. "It is the relative importance of tax, legal and general considerations which determine the 'best' structure for an LBO" (Michel & Shaked, 1988, p. 276).

However, the general concept of each holding structure is equal in all transactions. The LBO firm and other equity investors i.e. the target's actual management, or the target's future management found a joint acquisition vehicle. This acquisition vehicle acquires the company by using the equity provided by the founding parties and the debt borrowed by the banks. Hence, the target does not appear directly in the LBO fund's balance sheet but is solely listed as an equity investment in the respective holding. This structure eases the sale at a later point in time as well as the distribution of return. Furthermore, the holding structure sharply decreases the LBO fund's risk of becoming directly liable in case of a target's default. The holding structure is furthermore used to structural subordinate the debt used in the transaction's financial structure.

3.2.4 Financial Structure

With regard to the financial structure of a buyout, each form is financed through high gearing and a rather low equity stake. This superficial assumption is in line with the findings of Paulson (2001), who states that debt and mezzanine contribute 70 to 90% to the transaction sum (p. 143). Anyhow, each buyout exhibits its unique parameters, meaning that not every target is able to cope with the same gearing level and not every buyout fund is able, or willing to contribute the same amount of equity to the transaction. The trade-off between high returns caused by excessive leverage and increased default risk should be carefully evaluated.[5] Consequently, each buyout's financial structure must be developed individually.

However, since leverage serves as a tool to generate value in the buyout, the share of debt will be maximised with regard to the respective circumstances, and equity will only represent a fraction since its main purpose – besides the alignment of interest of the management team and the LBO fund – is to allocate the return generated through leverage to the entitled party. In terms of mezzanine, it plays a key strategic role in the buyout, yet in terms of funding, it has a minor role compared to the total amount of finance needed.

---

[5] This trade-off is discussed in more detail in section 4.1.1.

Referring back to the superficial statement that each buyout is financed through a large sum of debt and a fraction of equity, it holds, yet neglects the true complexity of the peculiarities used in a leveraged buyout.

In terms of debt, which serves as value driver, senior loans, subordinate loans, private placements and junk bonds play the primary role in buyouts. Usually, the major debt stake is contributed as senior and subordinate loan. Private placements as well as junk bonds[6] are only used in large transactions and hold a minor stake. With regard to the respective interest rates, senior loans receive the lowest, while junk bond holders receive the highest. This can be explained by the fact that with increasing risk, interest rates must rise.

Since the entire debt facility is solely secured by the target's assets, none of the lenders holds a claim against the LBO firm in case of insolvency (Neff, 2003, p. 42; Michel & Sharked, 1988, p. 244). Owing to this, the diverse lenders are ranked regarding their rights and settlement. Senior lenders' claims are met first. Afterwards, the subordinate lenders' claims are met, and if the amount generated through the liquidation still exceeds both lender groups' claims, private placements and junk bonds claimholders are paid. This structural subordination is, however, again dependant on the holding structure, for example while the senior facility is borrowed and secured directly by the target's operational business the high yield notes are usually issued by the holding.

The interest rate for senior and subordinate loans varies from 100 to 300 bp above the prime rate, yet the rate paid on the subordinate always exceeds the one of the senior facility (Graebner, 1991, p. 29; Michel & Shaked, 1988, p. 183; KKR, 1989, pp. 1-5). With regard to the rates paid for private placements and junk bonds, they vary strongly since the risk exposure differs from deal to deal, yet they are considerably higher than those paid on a subordinate facility (Altman, 2002, pp. 299-300).

Mezzanine has the purpose of aligning the interest of the parties involved and the purpose of increasing some parties' return in an LBO. It is a hybrid, since it is constructed through debt and equity, and it provides its holder with the equity's potential and a minimum level of debt's downside protection e.g. through interest payments (Michel & Shaked, 1988, p. 187; Graebner, 1991, p. 29).

Regarding equity in buyouts, common stock and preferred stock are used. Their proportion differs from deal to deal. While both forms represent ownership, their

---

[6] Bond specific risks are examined in section 4.3.4.

respective rights as well as their potential payoff differ. In terms of their return, both are priced according to the CAPM and in the case of a buyout can be considered as high risk investments yielding high returns. According to a study conducted by KKR, their fund generated an average annual return of 40% from 1976 to 1988 (KKR, 1989, p. 4). Besides the return, the holders of common stock have the chance to receive a dividend while the holder of preferred stock receives a cumulative payment, meaning that "unpaid dividends cumulate and must be paid in full before any dividends may be paid to holders of common stock" (Bodie, Kane & Marcus, 2005, p. 47).

As an example of the complex financial structure, the buyout of Macy's, America's ninth largest retailer back then, serves as an ideal example. The financial structure of the buyout was composed of $65m cash, $17.5m common stock, $282.5m preferred stock, $795m first senior loan paying prime rate plus 150 bp for the first five years and 50 bp for the last two years, $225m second senior loan with identical payoff structure, $15m revolving senior working capital loan, $800m mortgage backed loan paying 11% interest, $121.5m notes to insurance companies yielding 13.5% interest, $400m subordinate loan paying 14.5%, $450m private placements yielding 15.5%, $250m discount debentures with a coupon stating that 16.5% interest was paid after the senior facility had been paid off.

High returns of up to 16.5% on debt reflect the high risks involved for the lenders. This aspect sometimes is, however, neglected. There is no "free lunch".

3.3   Monitoring and Advising

After signing and closing of the acquisition the target becomes part of the LBO fund's portfolio and the monitoring and advising phase starts "in which the LBO firm swiftly exercises newly gained influence on managerial decisions of the buyout target" (Loos, 2006, p. 16). The LBO fund can either act as hands-on, or more common, as hands-off fund. While the former directly participates in the strategic and operational management of the portfolio company, the latter only provides guidance, yet allocates the responsibilities of the operational business to the portfolio company's management (Loos, 2006, p. 16; Kester & Luehrman, 1995, p. unknown). However, in each of the two strategy's, the LBO fund performs austerity programmes, actively manages both sides of the balance sheet and assures a change in financial focus of the company's management team from earnings to cash flow, and fosters growth (Loos, 2006, p. 16).

H. R. Kravis underlines the importance of the monitoring and advising phase in LBO transactions by stating:

"Once you buy a company, you are married. You are married to that company. It's a lot harder to sell a company than it is to buy a company. People always call and congratulate us when we buy a company. I say, 'look, don't congratulate us when we buy a company, congratulate us when we sell it. Because any fool can overpay and buy a company, as long as money will last to buy it.' Our job really begins the day we buy the company and we start working with the management, we start working with where this company is headed." (H. R. Kravis in Loos, 2006, p. 0)

With regard to the cash flow focus and austerity programmes, cost reductions are performed and the asset utilization is improved. In terms of the former, incentives as well as pressure for the top-management to generate higher cash flows and improve operating performance is increased[7], overhead cost are cut, firm's internal bureaucracy is minimized, decision making is accelerated and simplified, and corporate functions are made leaner (Loos, 2006, pp. 24-25).

Analysing the second, asset utilization is improved by increased control on corporate spending, acceleration of the collection of receivables, reduction of the inventory holding period, and extension of the payment period to suppliers (Bull, 1989; Anders, 1992; Holthausen & Larcker, 1996; Baker & Wruck, 1989)

In terms of active balance sheet management, the LBO Funds restructures both the portfolio firm's assets liabilities. Concerning the firm's assets, the fund "slashes unsound investment programmes and disposes assets that are unnecessary or underutilised" (Phan & Hill, 1995, p. 704). Regarding interest bearing liabilities, the buyout changes the entire financial structure.

3.4   Exit

The monitoring and advising phase ends with the planning of a divestment strategy, known as exit. The exit serves to sell the portfolio company – fully or partially – with the purpose to reduce risk exposure and to transform illiquid investments into realized returns (Povaly, 2007, p. 117). The exit is, in accordance with literature, timed two to five years after the closing has taken place (Gompers & Lerner, 1999, p. 246; Lerner & Hardymon, 2002; Bottazzi & Da Rin, 2002; Giot & Schwienbach, 2003). The planning

---

[7] See section 5.4 for an in-depth discussion on this issue.

of the exit begins with the identification of an exit opportunity (Lieber, 2004, p. 72). As a next step, the degree of exit must be decided, meaning that the fund has to decide whether they aim at conducting a full or a partial exit. Then, the exit strategy must be decided upon, with regard to the portfolio company's characteristics and its situation, the stock market's situation and the economic situation as whole, in order to assure that the most promising with regard to value is taken (Povaly, 2007, pp. 183-184). Furthermore, the process for each of these alternatives has distinct requirements with regard to size and characteristics of a portfolio company, execution timing, costs, public disclosure requirements and tax impact. With regard to the alternatives, five types of divestment routes must be taken into account, namely: trade sale, secondary buyout, initial public offering (IPO), buy-back, write-off and recapitalisation[8].

A trade sale or "M&A exit" is the sale of the portfolio company to an industry peer, a company positioned forward or backward in the value chain, or any other unrelated business (Kühn, 2005, p. 52). Hence, the buyer's motives are not purely financial but feature a strategic element since he aims at integrating the firm into its operational business and to realize synergies or profits from the firm's brand name, R&D, patents or else (Cumming& Macintosh, 2003b, p.117). In accordance with literature, a trade sale is seldom conducted as partial exit (Cumming & Macintosh, 2003a, p. 514; Polvary, 2007, p. 120).

In terms of the second divestment opportunity, the portfolio firm is sold to another LBO firm (Biggs, 2006, p. 143). "The concept is that another private equity house acquires a company, again structured as leveraged buyout" (Povaly, 2007, p. 110). Thus, in a secondary buyout, the acquiring firm has strictly financial motives and performs another highly geared acquisition.

In an IPO, the stock market is used as exit channel by selling the firm's shares to public investors. Through an IPO, the firm's ownership becomes liquid, since the shares are now publicly traded and usually more dispersed (Povaly, 2007, p. 122). Intrinsically, the conduction of an IPO is not an exit action but facilitates a following exit after the lock-up agreement has expired (Gompers & Learner, 1998, p. 2164; Cumming & Macintosh, 2003, p. 106). This is fact, because not the fund's entire ownership is sold through the

---

[8] Recapitalisation is not a divestment strategy in the narrow sense (Povaly; 2007, p. 118). However, in order to present the full set of opportunities, it is discussed in the paper. A recapitalisation is most prominent when the IPO market is in a down turn, and neither strategic nor financial investors show interest in the portfolio firm, while the LBO company faces pressure to repay their investors (Kushner, 2004, p. 97).

primary sale of shares in the IPO but after the lock-up period (Gompers & Learner, 1998, pp. 2164-2166). The IPO exit eliminates part of the return since firms are bought out at a premium and taken public with an IPO discount.

A buy-back transaction is an exit strategy in which the former seller represents the buyer, meaning that "a private equity fund sells its shares back to the company or entrepreneur that sold the shares originally" (Povaly, 2007, p. 124). A buy-back transaction is usually conducted if the former target has failed to achieve target financial values that were included in the acquisition contract (Cumming & Macintosh, 2003, p. 125).

A write-off, or liquidation, takes place when the portfolio firm is either 'walking wounded' or 'living dead'. In terms of the former, the company is performing poorly and the expected potential could not be realised (Povaly, 2007, p. 125). Here, the LBO firm might continue to hold the written-off ownership as "so-called lifestyle company that generates returns sufficient support to the entrepreneur in relative comfort but lacks sufficient upside potential to maintain the VC's[9] active involvement" (Cumming & Macintosh, 2003, p. 108). With regard to the latter, a 'living dead' company can be considered as a total failure. In this case, the only exit option is a raid.

In a recapitalisation the LBO firm's equity stake is partially reduced by taking up additional debt to finance the firm and paying an extraordinary dividend to the LBO firm to reduce the equity stake (Povaly, 2007, p. 125). Thus in an LBO recapitalisation, a fraction of the portfolio firm's equity is disbursed and replaced by new debt. "The idea is to increase the debt burden again on a portfolio firm that has already repaid a portion of the debt initially raised at the time of the acquisition" (Povaly, 2007, p. 125).

4   Risk Management in LBO Transactions

In this section, the focus lies on risks that are less considered in the public discussion. These include the consequences of high gearing ratios, the risks that previous bondholders encounter, and the risks to the financial system.

Three alternative approaches will be analysed with regard to the risk involved. The theoretical aspects will be presented first with a detailed definition of credit risk and its components. In this part, the credit risk of a bank as a creditor in an LBO transaction will be assessed. Furthermore, principal-agent theory will be applied to explain

---

[9] Cumming and Macintosh use the term VC (Venture Capital) as umbrella term to cover LBOs and Seed Finance.

additional risks created by differing interests on the agent (private equity fund) and the principal (bank financing an LBO deal). After, typical risks that are associated with a highly leveraged takeover as well as the consequences for the financial system will be subjected to analysis.

4.1   Credit Risk Implications for Lending Parties

Bessis (1998) defines credit risk as "the losses in the event of default of the borrower, or in the event of a deterioration of the borrower's credit quality" (p. 81). It can be divided into three components namely default, exposure, and recovery. When determining the credit risk it is essential to consider the quantity and the quality of a credit. The quantity is simply given by the amount a bank lends a private equity fund to finance its acquisition. The quality is determined by the probability of default and any type of guarantee that is part of the deal. The quantity or amount at risk usually differs from the actual loss in the case of a default due to possible recoveries. To summarise, the loss or credit risk can be compromised to the following equation (Bessis, 1998, pp. 81, 90):

$$Loss = default \times \exp osure \times (1 - re \cos ery)$$

For a bank involved in a leveraged buyout, these risks are fundamental and their assessment strongly determines whether a loan will be granted and which guarantees are expected. Therefore, the three components of credit risk will be briefly explained in the following sections.

Additionally, refinancing has become significantly more expensive for banks due to the credit crunch and the extraordinary volatility in the EURIBOR and LIBOR as well as other spreads. Although the situation has been eased by the liquidity intervention of €200bn by the European Central Bank, nobody can predict at what point in time credit markets will behave "normally" again. This aspect certainly impacts current LBO developments and has forced many buyout firms to put their projects on hold.

4.1.1   Default Risk

Theoretically, a default can be triggered by various events that must not necessarily be threatening to the solvency of the borrower. A payment default, for instance, is usually declared if a scheduled payment has not been serviced within three months of the agreed date. This is the timeframe that rating agencies mainly use to define a default. A technical default is given when the debtor violates a covenant, such as a predetermined financial ratio. Depending on the contract between debtor and creditor and without waivers granted by the lender, a technical default can instantly lead to the bankruptcy of the borrower since he may be obliged to repay the outstanding sum immediately. An economic default occurs when the present value of expected cash flows generated by the assets employed is inferior to the outstanding debt. This form of default can not be as closely monitored since the value of assets and cash flow expectations fluctuate in line with market conditions. Nevertheless, an economic default is still highly relevant (Bessis, 1998, p. 82).

Rating agencies determine default risk on the basis of historical data and statistical probability. Investment grade borrowers have an historical annual default rate of up to 1%. All other debtors are regarded as being speculative and have rates superior to 1%. It is, however, important to note that the probability of default increases significantly with a longer time period. Default rates are strictly annual observations which add up the longer the time horizon is. (Bessis, 1998, pp. 90-93).

4.1.2 Exposure Risk

This type of risk becomes especially relevant if the debtor is granted a certain line of credit which he can draw upon at any time. Consequently, the creditor has difficulty estimating his exposure at different points in time. In the case of a credit line the amount of exposure to a bank is, hence, not predictable. A problem associated with this kind of risk is its off-balance sheet recording since it is a matter of probability whether the credit will be utilised (Bessis, 1998, pp. 84, 95).

In the case of fixed repayment schedules, the exposure is always clearly defined. Since LBO transactions are financed at once, the exposure risk is usually not of major importance for the private equity – bank relationship. Nevertheless, incidences where an LBO target is granted a credit line for its operational business are not unlikely.

4.1.3 Recovery Risk

Recovery risk relates to the risk that an outstanding loan cannot be fully repaid by a lender in the case of default. The amount of money that can be recovered depends on the different forms of guarantees if the collateral base is depleted in case of default. Guarantees are arranged as collateral, covenants and/or third-party guarantees. With collaterals it again depends on the specific type of collateral. Cash has no recovery risk associated with it. From this point on, the risk increases with a decreasing degree of liquidity. Financial assets of any kind are still preferred over fixed assets such as real estate, planes or ships. The value of the collateral can also be volatile with changing market prices. Consequently, the quality of a credit that has been mentioned at the beginning relates to the underlying collateral (Bessis, 1998, pp. 84-85).

Covenants have the advantage that they allow the lender to engage in proactive risk management before a default occurs. In order to keep their value as high as possible, a close credit risk monitoring has to be installed. Third-party guarantees on the other hand can be viewed as a passive measure that functions as insurance in a default. The risk is shared between the debtor and the guarantor. They are subject to a joint default probability which will be significantly lower since the individual probabilities are multiplied. If the guarantor and the lender are, however, not independent of each other with regard to their company structure, this advantage is no longer existent. Additionally, there are legal risks involved since a recovery through a third-party is not always easy to enforce. This issue can be especially painful for the creditor because all commitments of the debtor are suspended until all legal issues are resolved (Bessis, 1998, pp. 85, 97-98). Any costs e.g. legal fees or opportunity costs while waiting for payments that relate to the recovery on the side of the lender have to be included in the overall loss of a default.

A possible severe downturn of the LBO activity triggered by several large defaults could ultimately lead to a sharp increase of recovery risk. A vicious circle may develop, where instability of the private equity industry quickly increases when banks hold back credits for further transactions.

4.2   Principal Agent Conflict between Lender and LBO Firm

One, among various other principal agent conflicts that arise in an LBO is the difference in objectives between the bank, as principal, and the equity investor as agent. This conflict of interest originates in the unequal risk return payoff structure of the two actors. The private equity firm maximises its utility by levering the target company as high as possible. The higher the amount of debt capital, the higher the return on equity will be. Therefore, the agent would leverage its firm above the underlying collateral in order to pursue its desired return rate. This will especially hold as soon as the liquidation value of the bought enterprise is equal or lower than the outstanding debt. In that case, the equity investor's loss is capped on the downside but he still has much potential on the upside if the deal succeeds.

The principal tries to restrict the debt since he wants to keep his exposure under control. The creditor's interest rate is usually fixed and not adjustable for an increased default risk. In order to keep the risk manageable, the principal will have difficulties to accept an exposure above the collateral base since the resulting risk will be over-proportional. As opposed to the agent, the principal's return or upside is capped but his downside risk can go as far as to lose the complete loan in the case of bankruptcy (Michel & Shaked, 1988, p. 244-247).

Kessel (1995) translates this conflict of interest into the asset substitution and the claim dilution problem. A private equity fund invests its debt and equity capital into high-risk enterprises and once a company is bought, the operative measures in the time period until the exit are also risky. This fact is not surprising since high returns that have been generated by the private equity industry in recent years must have been accompanied by high risks. Without high yields for the investing companies, the private equity business model would not hold since only the returns that exceed the debt payments are profits for the owners. The consequences of the asset substitution problem for the principal can best be described in form of a European long call option held by the agent and a short call option on the side of the principal. Theoretically, the principal buys the company with its loan and the agent receives the debt capital plus an option on the company's assets as the purchase price. The agent therefore has an option, not an obligation, to sell back the enterprise on the expiry date. The strike price of the long call option is equivalent to the amount of debt service. Once the value[10] of the company exceeds the strike price, the option is "in the money" and it will be profitable for the agent to exercise it. If not, the agent would let the option expire meaning that the LBO transaction would have failed. This scenario relates to the differing risk structures of the agent and the principal examined earlier. Due to his limited downside risk, the agent will invest without risk aversion which is not in the interest of the principal (Kessel, 1995, pp. 63-77; Forst, 1993, pp. 120-122).

Just as the asset substitution problem, the claim dilution problem also relates to issues that have already been touched before. Claim dilution refers to the possibility that the agent can opportunistically influence the interest paid on debt. As mentioned, LBO

---

[10] Value of the company defined as the value of its assets and the cash flows generated by the assets

loans by banks are usually negotiated with a fixed interest rate or at least with a fixed risk premium. If the agent further leverages his company with additional senior debt, the exposure risk in the case of a default for the principal increases without being reflected through higher returns. The degree of this effect certainly depends on whether the principal is a senior or subordinate lender. Nevertheless, the claim dilution problem exists for all previous claim holders in the case of additional debt. Informational asymmetries between the agent and the principal are the primary cause for this dilemma. A special group affected by this are bondholders and in some cases the entire bond market. This issue will be addressed in the next section.

4.3   Typical Risk Factors to the Target and its Stakeholders

Up to now the risks on the side of the lender of an LBO transaction and possible theoretical explanations for the occurrence of these risks have been discussed. In this chapter, the focus will be on the target company's risks. The areas that will be examined are operational risks, such as a negligence of long term investments, and the risk involved for previous bondholders as well as the bond market as a whole.

4.3.1   Operational Risks Caused by Buyout Firm Misbehaviour

Especially in Germany, private equity funds do not enjoy a good reputation partly triggered by thoughtless politicians who denounced the whole industry as Heuschrecken (Die Zeit, 2005). This criticism mainly relates to the view of the general public that private equity companies buy domestic firms with the aim to maximise their own profit in a short period of time and thereby totally neglect operational duties. This may cause sufferance to the target firm long after the exit of the investor. The situation is, however, more complex. Private equity funds usually sell their companies at a higher price than initially bought. The following investor therefore has to value the enterprise higher than it was before. An essential part of value creation for the buyout firm is certainly financial engineering. Nevertheless, a successful exit will not be possible if the capital structure is the only aspect that has been restructured. In fact, studies proof that on average buyout targets experience an increase in their EBITDA, a performance measassurement not influenced by the capital structure (Kaplan, 1989, p. 26). Lichtenberg and Siegel (1990) also demonstrate that the productivity of these firms increases with a buyout (pp. 36-40).

A further risk that may only show its effects after a longer period of time is the decrease of long term investments such as R&D. The reason for such cuts appear to be obvious since a buyout firm is dependent on a high cash flow and cutting on research costs may be an easy measure to increase short-term cash flows. Although the study is not representative, KKR (1989) showed for 17 of its portfolio companies that the expenditures on R&D decreased in the first year after the takeover but exceeded the previous level afterwards. A negligence of research efforts is hereby not proven (pp. 1-8).

Finally, downsizing of the workforce and closing of business units is probably the most popular criticism. Publicly recognised negative examples of failed LBO transactions such as Grohe[11] add to this perception (Köhn, 2005). Kaplan (1989), however, has found that the workforce of targeted companies actually increases by 4.9% (p. 26). In many cases, employees have to be made redundant to increase the scope of action for management at first; however, with the result that more people join the company later. This tactic easily leads to a misperception in public since 1,000 fired workers are more media-effective than 1,000 hired employees.

A further prejudice is the closing down of entire business units. However, business divisions are rather sold off than closed down. The former is a convenient method to generate cash which is essential since many buyout deals fail due to illiquidity according to Lichtenberg & Siegel (1990, p. 29-30). Besides, no buyout firm can protect its portfolio firm against operational risks in the form of external changes such as higher competitive pressure or changing customer desires (Paprottka, 1996, p. 63).

In conclusions, most prejudice towards private equity funds could be proven wrong. The fulfilment of cash flow expectations, low interest rates and leverage risk have a significantly higher importance and could even affect the whole financial system as described below.

4.3.2   Leverage Risk Implications

So far an operative mismanagement and risks to stakeholders of the target firm or the buyout firm have been examined. The main reason for the failure of LBO transactions is, however, the leverage risk. On the one hand, a private equity fund needs a high

---

[11] Grohe was taken private by BC Partners and sold to TPG and Credit Suisse First Boston Private Equity in a secondary buyout. The new owners made one third of all German employees redundant (1,500 in total) and took €500m of equity out of the company. This incident occurred during the political Heuschrecken-debate and was, hence, heavily discussed. (Köhn, 2005)

gearing ratio to achieve its desired returns with the help of the leverage effect. On the other hand, high debt-to-equity ratios can be difficult to compensate for the target firm. The cash flows generated strongly determine the possible debt amortisation and interest payments and hence the possible amount of leverage. Any changes in the projected economic environment of the company or a change in interest rates can quickly lead to illiquidity (Kessel, 1991, pp. 40-41). Scenario analyses are used to determine the maximum potential gearing ratio. These analyses range from a worst case over a most likely to a best case scenario and the generated free cash flow is always the primarily observed factor. Like any scenario analysis these are based on assumptions. The assumptions of the investor can easily be biased and do not always reflect an objective reality. Consequently, some LBO projects are tightly calculated to yield a maximum return for the investor. The slightest complications in such projects can, therefore, rapidly lead to default. An example of such a scenario analysis is given below (Baker & Smith, 2006, p. 125).

One of the most prominent examples of a failed LBO caused by a too aggressive gearing ratio is the takeover of the American drug store chain Revco D. S. in December 1986. The $1.4 billion deal was financed with an amazing $1.267 billion in debt, $188m in mezzanine and only $35m in equity capital leading to an extraordinary pure debt-to-equity ratio of 36.2. Nineteen month after the deal, Revco filed for court protection under Chapter 11 of the Bankruptcy Code. Clearly the assumptions of future cash flows were far too optimistic and the entire financial engineering was too aggressive. An analysis conducted after the failure of the deal concluded that the probability of success was estimated to be between five and 30% (Bruner, 2005, pp. 127-145).

To conclude, the financial package by the buyout firm strongly determines the success of the transaction. The buyout fund finds itself in a dilemma in every deal. On the one hand the fund wants to achieve its targeted returns; on the other hand overly aggressive gearing can quickly lead to default. The optimal balance and realistic expectations of future cash flows are primary success factors.

4.3.3   Excursus: Scenario Analysis

In order to assess the implications a variation in interest rates or cash flow has on the default probability, a simplified scenario analysis is conducted. The conservative scenario one consists of a 100m LBO transaction funded with 70% debt. The average interest rate is set at 10% and the expected revenues amount to $160m with a resulting free cash flow of \$26.4m. The targeted exit horizon is five years. This base scenario leads to a delta or safety net of \$5.4m in the first year and rising further on.[12] The first alteration (scenario two) is – ceteris paribus – an increase of the gearing level to an 80% debt portion. Consequently the return on equity increases but the delta is reduced to \$2.4m in year one due to the higher financial burden. The following scenarios will all be based on the 80% debt level.

Similarly, in scenario three, the effects of higher interest rates have been examined by an increase of 200 bp to 12%. Considering the recent volatility in the iTraxx Europe index such an increase is realistic (iTraxx, 2007). This alteration can still be absorbed but the safety net becomes fairly thin with \$800,000 in the first year.

Scenario four tests the impact of lower cash flows than expected at the original interest rate of 10%. The future revenues are by far the most difficult assumptions that have to be made in an LBO model. A variation of revenues can be caused by a collapse in demand or simply because of wrong expectations. In the analysis, a reduction of revenues to \$150m with a free cash flow of 24m eliminates the delta to zero in the first year. In the following four years, however, the safety net stabilises with a yearly increase of \$800,000.

Finally, in the last scenario (five), the effects of both an interest rate rise and fewer cash flows are examined. In this case, the last two distortions (12% interest rate and \$150m revenues) are combined. The safety net becomes negative (-\$1,600,000) and hence the LBO runs into default.

The different scenarios demonstrate how quickly the tightly calculated LBO deals can run into serious trouble if unexpected external events occur. Regarding the current economic developments that have been drastically described at the beginning, especially scenario five has to be taken serious by deal makers. Often buyout firms build their forecasts on either a disturbance in interest rates or cash flows but hardly both combined. Even though a transaction may be prudently calculated, external influences can always lead to default.

4.3.4   Losses for Previous Bondholders

The risk implications for creditors of a buyout target have already been discussed in detail. In this part, the focus is on bondholders and the effects they encounter through a

---

[12] Cf Appendix for more details.

leveraged buyout. The loss for previous corporate bondholders manifests itself through a sharp decrease in the value of publicly traded bonds of the particular company on the day of the deal announcement. It is especially problematic that this event risk is hard to estimate and is not included in a rating such as the classical credit risk. Assuming that bondholders keep their notes until maturity, their return is not affected but it is still an unrealised loss. The decrease of bond prices is just the symptom of the underlying problem. The fundamental change of the capital structure increases the default risk for bondholders and their returns do not get adjusted to the higher risk. This is the issue bondholders are confronted with; whereas equity holders mainly benefit from a take-over, bondholders usually suffer (Markey, 1989, p. 213).

In the light of more LBO deals in recent years, bondholders have started to demand more protection. One possibility to assure bondholders are event risk covenants which have become popular again in the 1980s. One form are change over control covenants. This special form of covenant is designed to give bondholders a compensation for the credit deterioration in the case of a takeover by stating that the financing of an acquisition must not decrease the issuer's creditworthiness. The increasing popularity of change over control covenants can be traced back to the 1988 RJR Nabisco take-over by KKR where bondholders suffered a one billion dollar loss caused by a 20% drop in bond notations (Ross, Westerfield & Jaffe, 2005, pp. 497-501).

Another form of protection was demanded by investors in April 2007. Estée Lauder could only issued its $600m commercial bond because it finally gave in on market demands and granted investors a change of control put for the case of a takeover. Otherwise, it was estimated, that the company would have had to pay an extra 20 bp[13]. Nevertheless, the mentioned puts are often based at par[14] which is not very helpful for investors with papers trading well above 100. Such a put is regularly granted to bondholders in case their conditions of a change over control covenant are violated (Durand, 2007, p. 107; Euromoney, 2006, pp.12-14).

An alternative approach to bondholder protection was introduced by Citigroup in 2006. They designed a new product called Significant Acquisition and Increased Leverage Swaption (Sails). It is constructed in a way that the value of the swaption increases in line with an increase in spreads, giving investors a hedge. However, the real innovation

---

[13] Estée Lauder issued a $600m 10 and 30 year SEC-registered bond. The estimated spread premium for the 10 year tranche was 10 bp and 30 bp for the 30 year tranche.
[14] A bond trades at par when its price equals 100. In this situation the yield equals the nominal interest.

compared to plain vanilla CDS swaptions[15] is a protection against aggressive leveraging measured through a debt-to-EBITDA ratio, for instance. A change in this ratio influences the value of the Sail just as much as a change in spreads. According to Citigroup, the new product is primarily aimed at bond investors who wish to hedge themselves against LBO risk (Euroweek, 2006, p. 12). Similarly, in the recent LBO of First Data through KKR in September 2007, KKR gave in on demands to include a debt-to-EBITDA ratio covenant to the senior debt holders.

The financing of highly leveraged deals has, of course, been heavily influenced by the credit crunch this summer. Some sources estimate that $330bn of leverage buyout debt are waiting to be processed through the credit market. One of the largest deals in the pipeline is the $54bn buyout of TXU Corp. through KKR and TPG. According to Fitch Ratings' the involved companies need to issue $26bn in loans and $11bn in bonds. Another example is the $26.3bn LBO of the wireless operator Alltel Communications by TPG and GS Capital Partners (High Yield Report, 2007, pp. 1-8).

The boom in the M&A market and the LBO transactions as a part of it has made all bondholders nervous. Club deals have shown that even large investment grade enterprises are not safe. Consequently, investors are more cautious and demanding. The British airport operator BAA almost completed the issue of a €2.85bn bond transaction but rumours about Spain's Grupo Ferrovial taking over BAA totally changed the situation. The company had to guarantee its bondholders protection and the conditions of the issue had to be changed in the last minute (Euromoney, 2006, pp. 12-14).

In the end, especially private equity companies are dependent on bonds to refinance themselves. This might also be a reason why bond investors were treated very fairly in the LBO of Danish telecom TDC (Whitehouse, 2005, pp. 1-4). Nevertheless, measures to protect bondholders are likely to gain further importance in the future. In Denmark – and this might be a reason for the fair treatment of bondholders in the TDC transaction – in accordance with the Danish Public Companies Act Sec. 115 (2) companies are very limited with regard to financial assistance. The Danish regulators prohibit firms the use of loans to finance the acquisitions of their own shares. Besides various forms of covenants, an increased disclosure of information for bondholders could be a measure to offer this group of investors higher transparency. A possible negative aspect of

---

[15] A CDS swaption is an option on a credit default swap. This form of credit derivative has only recently become popular. Calls and puts are traded on CDSs and cancellable CDSs, the latter containing an embedded option to terminate an existing CDS.

covenants is that they limit the scope of action of management. In some cases it may be beneficial for all stakeholders of a company if the financial structure is changed. Covenants restrict the flexibility of the management and a weaker company performance is certainly not desired by bondholders. It is a thin trade-off between sufficient protection from event risk and necessary flexibility.

4.4   Risks to the Financial System

Besides the risks to investors and companies involved, LBO transactions account for serious risks to the international financial system as a whole. The somehow instable state of the LBO market with regard to too optimistic cash flow expectations and increasing volatile interest rates has already been discussed in a worst case scenario at the beginning. A default of a large firm which has experienced a leveraged buyout could be a trigger for a downturn of the whole industry. If banks lose confidence in LBO transactions, they might quickly stop financing. Additionally, they could hold back bridge loans and secondary financing of LBO targets which may lead to the default of firms that would have succeeded otherwise. The recent subprime crisis has demonstrated how quickly investors lose confidence and how one crisis can lead to another. Hence, a number of defaults could affect the entire credit market with less liquidity as just experienced as a result. The Bank of England supports this view by stating that LBO activities led to an overall increase of the insolvency probability of all British firms by 0.2%. They estimate that several smaller and bigger LBO defaults are inevitable in the coming years (Morgan, 2006, p. 11). The same applies for Germany where defaults of several billion Euros are expected by experts of the industry (Maier, 2006). The occurrence probability of this scenario is, of course, unlikely but still some parallels between the subprime crisis and the LBO market can be drawn. Both yielded their investors extremely high returns for years which might have led to a neglecting of the risk involved. A medium for such a drastic development could be a generally insecure market as today with the threat of a downturn of consumer spending and GDP growth rates in the US. All participants of the LBO market should be aware of the mentioned risks to the financial system but if this makes them act more carefully is questionable. This fact may lead to a necessity of higher regulations in the LBO sector to prevent the industry from crashing. Means that regulate those issues belong to the field of corporate governance and will be assessed in the next chapter.

5   Governance Implications in Leveraged Financed Deals

Corporate governance became a topic of major importance in the last few years. The Enron scandal[16] in the end of 2001 and the WorldCom case in the middle of 2002 (Tanski, 2002, p. 2003) demonstrated impressively the insufficiency of the existing governance mechanisms in the United States. Not only the US but also European countries realised that their corporate governance systems did not work properly.[17] Moreover, there is also an ongoing debate about private equity companies and a discussion about the need for stronger regulations in the private equity market. The recent Heuschreckendebatte (Die Zeit, 2005) in Germany showed a lack of competitiveness of the German capital market, but also suggested amendments in the German corporate governance system. This debate has led to rising attention on the activities of private equity investors and has set up the question of whether tougher governance policies are necessary.

This chapter will examine the fundamentals and recent changes in both the American and the German corporate governance system and discuss their impact on private equity firms and leveraged finance deals. In a next step, further governance implications concerning the principal-agent relationship between management and shareholders will be discussed. Thus, a strong focus will be on the free cash flow hypothesis (Jensen, 1986) and the impact of corporate governance mechanism on value increase in leveraged buyouts.

5.1   The American Corporate Governance System

5.1.1   The Legal Form of a Corporation

A corporation, the American equivalent of the German "Aktiengesellschaft", consists of three bodies namely the shareholder meeting, the board of directors and the officers. Shareholders elect the board of directors which in turn appoints the officers. In this so-called monistic or one-tier model, there is a strong personal interdependence between the board of directors and the officers, i.e. there are often officers who act as board members. In US-corporations, the board is traditionally divided into two groups which are executive and non-executive directors. Executive board members manage the

---

[16] Cf. Frentz, 2003, p. 1 for a chronic on the Enron case
[17] E.g. the Suisse Adecco S.A. was not able to publish its annual result for 2003 on January 12, 2004 due to lacks in its internal control system. The adjournment sine die resulted in a 47% share price drop (cf. Hamburger Abendblatt, 13.01.2004).

company whereas non-executive directors supervise the management (PwC & BDI, 2005).

In order to understand the American corporate governance system, it is essential to have profound knowledge of the relations between the different bodies of a corporation. Especially in the last decade, the relationship between management, control and corporate success became of greater importance to the shareholders. In the US, shareholder interests are often based on the expectations of short-term oriented institutional investors. In order to correct the strong interdependencies between officers and the board and to shift power to the shareholders, investors hold extensive rights to sue the company. The advantage of this aspect of the US governance system is that it reduces information asymmetries between management and the controlling body.

5.1.2   The Securities and Exchange Commission

Another important institution in the US governance system is the Securities and Exchange Commission (SEC). The SEC was founded in 1934 as a reaction to the changes in the US capital market law associated with the introduction of both the Securities Act of 1933 and the Securities Exchange Act of 1934. The main objectives of the SEC are to protect investors, maintain fair, orderly, and efficient markets, and facilitate capital formation on a federal level (SEC, 2007). According to Skousen (1991), the SEC shall contribute to capital market efficiency by means of "full and fair disclosure of all material facts concerning securities offered for public investment" (p. 7). As a strong and powerful organisation, the SEC is able to sanction corporations if they do not comply with its rules and guidelines (Pellens et al., 2004, p. 57).

5.1.3   The Sarbanes-Oxley Act of 2002

Not only the SEC but also the US legislature plays an important role in setting corporate governance regulations. As a response to a number of major corporate and accounting scandals including those affecting Enron and WorldCom, the Sarbanes-Oxley Act of 2002 (SOA) was signed into law by President George W. Bush who referred to the act as "the most far-reaching reform of American business practices since the time of Franklin D. Roosevelt." (Bumiller, 2002, p. A1). The above mentioned scandals led to a decline of public trust in accounting and reporting practices. In order to correct the deficiencies of the existing corporate governance system, the SOA established new or enhanced standards for all US public company boards, management, and public accounting firms. A remarkable aspect of the SOA is the fact that it does not primarily focus on the strengthening of shareholder interests but rather on imposing further responsibilities on corporations and auditors. Nevertheless, the SOA also includes new disclosure responsibilities (Menzies, 2004, p. 13).

Besides the stated fields of impact, the SOA affects private equity companies. Private equity funds often seek board representation in connection with their investments in order to play a more active role in the portfolio company's management, strategic development and direction. The SOA and the amended listing standards of the NYSE and Nasdaq will affect the composition of the board of directors and audit committees[18] of certain portfolio companies and will impact the individual members of the board. Boiled down to its essence, these requirements make it difficult for most private equity sponsors to have their representatives serve on audit committees of listed companies. This is because private equity firms will frequently hold more than 10% of those companies, but they will have more influence in terms of overall board representation and service on compensation and nominating committees (Warner & Ceberio, 2004).

In addition to far reaching independence requirements, there are further regulations imposed by the SOA which affect private equity companies. SOA forces companies to obey further disclosure obligations. Especially the assessment and reporting on internal controls (cf. Section 404 SOA) leads to an enormous increase in compliance costs and does not add commensurate benefit to a corporation. Furthermore, Warner and Ceberio (2004) argue that companies must disclose any off-balance sheet arrangements which currently have or are reasonably likely to have a material future impact on the company. In addition, it is prohibited publishing any non-GAAP or pro-forma financial measure unless it also presents the most directly comparable GAAP measure along with a quantitative reconciliation of non-GAAP to GAAP measure.

According to Akin Gump (2003), extensions or maintenance of credit, or arrangements to extend credit through personal loans by a corporation to any executive officer or director of the company, have been prohibited as of July 30, 2002. This rule can have an impact for portfolio companies that are or might go public or file a registration statement in respect of a bond exchange offer. This restriction inhibits the ability of

---

[18] Section 301 SOA requires the establishment of an audit committee. The audit committee shall supervise the adequate and orderly accounting and control the selection and compensation of the auditor (Menzies, 2004, p. 18).

private equity sponsors to lend money to management to facilitate equity participation by management. This affects particularly outstanding loans that need to be repaid prior to the filing of a registration statement to go public or to register a bond exchange offer in order to comply with Sarbanes-Oxley.

In conclusion, the changes due to the implementation of the SOA do not have a dramatic impact on how private equity firms operate. However, private equity investors must care about the changes made, in order to avoid liability, adverse media selection or reputation risk. Therefore, sponsors should ensure that each of their portfolio companies acts in accordance with the SOA regulations in order to develop a "compliance culture" (Warner & Ceberio, 2005).

5.2   The German Corporate Governance System

5.2.1   The Legal Form of the Aktiengesellschaft

As mentioned above, the German counterpart of a corporation is the Aktiengesellschaft (AG) which is subject to most corporate governance regulations in Germany. The AG is characterised by a so-called dualistic or two-tier model which is based on a strict division between the board of directors (Vorstand) and the supervisory board (Aufsichtsrat). The dualistic model of a German AG features the independence of its bodies. The board of directors is the executive management body of the corporation whereas the supervisory board appoints the board members and controls the activities of the board (PwC & BDI, 2005). The shareholder meeting in turn has the duty to elect the members of the supervisory board. However, the shareholder rights in Germany are very limited compared to the US. They are entitled to receive a dividend and can demand information from the board of directors. Moreover, they decide how to use the net profit for the year and discharge the management board, but they do not hold as extensive rights as shareholders in the US.

5.2.2   The Development of the German Corporate Governance System

Over the last years, the development of a German corporate governance system was highly influenced by the demands of the capital market. Especially Anglo-Saxon investors requested good principles for corporate governance while criticising the intransparent body of different legislations in Germany (e.g. AktG, HGB and WpHG). It was almost impossible to compare the German system on an international level. From an investor's point of view, major disadvantages of the German governance system were the restrictive information policies of German corporations. Due to the fact that the international capital market has a high demand for information, the question arose how to design a transparent governance system in Germany (Dörner & Orth, 2003, pp. 13-14).

The study of PwC and BDI (2005) mentions several legislative acts which aim at improving the German corporate governance system (p. 22). Due to the limited scope of the topic, this paper will only briefly describe the development of the German corporate governance system without a detailed discussion of the different acts which where signed into law in recent years.[19] The first important step towards the internationalisation of the German corporate governance system was the introduction of the "Kapitalaufnahmeerleichterungsgesetz" (KapAEG) (BGBl. I, 1998, p. 707) and of the "Gesetz zur Kontrolle und Transparenz im Unternehmensbereich (KonTraG) (BGBl. I, 1998, p. 786) in May 1998. Additional measures to improve the German corporate governance system have been taken with the implementation of the German Corporate Governance Code in February 2002 and the "Transparenz- und Publizitätsgesetz" (TransPuG) in July 2002. The years between 2003 and 2005 were characterised by the implementation of the "Maßnahmenkatalog zur Stärkung der Unternehmensintegrität und des Anlegerschutzes" (so-called 10-Punkte Plan). This plan consists of ten points which are influenced by Anglo-Saxon corporate governance concepts. The major aspects of the program aim, like the SOA does, at an increase of obligations for both the board of directors and the supervisory board. In addition, there are further improvements in other fields of the German governance system e.g. the implementation of a two-stage enforcement system in order to secure adequate and orderly accounting (BGBl. I, 2004, pp. 3408-3409) or increased independence requirements for auditors in the "Bilanzrechtsreformgesetz" (BilReG) (BGBl. I, 2004, pp. 3166-3167).

All those measures aim at a strengthening of investors' trust in capital markets. The modernisation of the German corporate governance system followed suit of the Anglo-Saxon governance system. It is obvious that the different international governance systems are converging due to an increasing interdependence of capital markets worldwide. Hence, a German system which is more investor oriented will be doubtlessly to the benefit of private equity companies. Nevertheless, the German private

---

[19] For a detailed description on the development of the German corporate governance system in recent years, cf. PwC & BDI, 2005, pp. 22.

equity market is still small compared to that in other countries like the USA or the UK.[20] Therefore, it can be expected that the German legislator will pass further regulations that target on increasing the competitiveness of the German capital market in order to attract more foreign investors.[21] In this context, the risk of running into a trade-off situation between investor orientation and creditor protection should not be neglected.

5.3   Creditor Protection in LBO Transactions

The recent developments in the American and German corporate governance systems show different tendencies in the attitude towards creditors. In the US, on the one hand, further restrictions and obligations were put on companies and in particular on the management in order to improve the existing governance mechanisms. Germany on the other hand, developed a market oriented corporate governance regime which focuses on increasing transparency and international competitiveness.

An important issue in the discussion about LBO transactions and their associated risks is the efficient protection of creditors. As already mentioned, LBO firms will maximise leverage. Consequently, the risk of insolvency increases and, hence, the probability of default. In an LBO situation, the target company is the debtor and usually the private equity company itself is excluded from liability for its portfolio companies. Therefore, without sufficient creditor protection, opportunistic behaviour of debtors and the private equity firms prevails. Due to that, an LBO is a "prototype" of a creditor exposure. Since the LBO market might find itself at a crossroad with one way leading to a severe downturn as described in various scenarios above, the need for creditor protection through regulations is urgent. The negative development in the late 1980s where 22 out of 83 transactions faced financial difficulties as opposed to only two out of 41 between 1980 and 1984 must be prevented (Kaplan & Stein, 1993).

In Germany, the balance sheet based capital maintenance rule prohibits the payout of any equity except for retained earnings. In the case of a merger, which is a possible way to conduct an LBO, this method is not necessarily applicable and can consequently weaken creditor protection. To increase creditor rights, the application of cash flow

---

[20] E.g. gross investments of private equity firms in Germany amounted to 0,12% of the GDP in 2004 whereas this figure was 0,85% in the UK (Sachverständigenrat, 2005, p. 464).
[21] The proposed amendment to the "Gesetz zur Modernisierung der Rahmenbedingungen für Kapitalbeteiligungen" (MoRaG) which will be signed into law on January 1, 2008 can be regarded as an example for this intention.

oriented solvency tests is a common method in this situation. Solvency tests are also widely used in Anglo-Saxon countries. According to this method, the financial burden of the target must not exceed future cash flows derived with a prudent estimation. A major difference between the two methods lies in their time orientation. Whereas the balance sheet based capital maintenance rule is based on past figures, solvency tests are future oriented.

The pros and cons of the two methods have been controversially discussed lately. According to an anonymous paper, which compared both methods with regard to their level of creditor protection, the balance sheet based capital maintenance rule is superior. The study shows that in 87% of all cases observed, the solvency test allows significantly higher new indebtedness. Therefore, the solvency test regime causes a higher damage to creditors than in the balance sheet based capital maintenance regime.

Another critical aspect of the solvency test is the prediction of future cash flows based on management expectations. From a creditor's perspective, it is difficult to verify those estimates. In case of a complete regime change, an independent controlling entity would be necessary to monitor management's predictions. Therefore, the objectivity of all management's assumptions is essential. The need for monitoring relates to the superior principal agent conflict between management and ownership.

5.4 Separation of Power and Control and the Free Cash Flow Hypothesis

Discussing governance mechanisms always involves an examination of the relationship between management and shareholders. In particular, this inside relationship of a corporation is essential in LBO transactions because there are certain principal-agent conflicts prevailing. Thus, this paragraph asserts the impact of governance mechanisms on value increase in leveraged buyouts.

In a typical LBO transaction, the shares of a publicly listed company are bought out with debt and the firm is delisted, becoming a private corporation owned by a limited number of outside investors and often the firm's top management. DeAngelo et al. (1984) found that in such transactions the pre-buyout stockholders of target firms earn abnormal gains of 30 to 80%. This empirical fact gives rise to the question why private equity companies pay a significant higher price than the current market value for LBO targets.

An answer can be found in the characteristics of the target firm that are different from those of firms remaining public. Loos (2006) argues that LBO firms act as intermediaries between the shareholders (i.e. the investors in an LBO fund) and the top management of the target company (p. 14). Because LBO firms are organised as private partnerships and not as public corporations, the LBO firm must be regarded as a hybrid between managers (agents) and owners (principals). From a corporate governance point of view, this will have a significant impact on the behaviour of the management and, hence, can increase the efficiency of the target company. In addition, Baker and Montgomery (1994) found that the incentive structure of LBO fund managers is such that there is almost a complete incentive alignment between them and the owners. Nevertheless, since managers are often financially involved in a buyout, their risk judgement is easily clouded by the desired high returns and limited downside risk.

According to Jensen (1986), LBO transactions increase firm value because the governance structure in LBOs provides stronger incentives for management to operate the company more efficiently than does the governance structure of a public corporation. It is generally accepted that managers in the latter case do not have strong incentives to allocate corporate resources in a way that shareholders' wealth is maximised (Sappington, 1983). First, large corporations tend to have large numbers of small shareholders who have only small incentives to monitor managers' decisions due to their relatively low amount invested into the company (Shleifer & Vishny, 1986). This situation leads to inefficiencies because intervention by diffuse shareholders is costly and is subject to free-rider problems. In the late 1980s, wrong incentives were set to managers. Instead of rewarding managers for sustainable profits, they often received incentives for the size of the corporation which led to extensive empire building (Jensen & Murphy, 1989). Therefore, managers tended to invest stockholders' funds in diversification or expansion in order to increase their personal wealth but this does not increase the firms' market value. If generated free cash flow is not invested in profitable development of the business or distributed to the shareholders, agency costs of free cash flow arise.

According to Jensen's free cash flow hypothesis (1986), LBOs result in corporate governance mechanisms that reduce agency costs and increase firm value through operating efficiency. Debt, ownership of equity and the presence of active investors are the main elements of this governance structure. High leverage reduces these agency costs by means of substituting dividends because this creates an obligation to service periodic interest costs. The company faces liquidation if it is not able to service these payments. Due to the fact that gearing in buyouts tends to be high, a significant portion is likely to be committed to service the debt. Nikoskelainen and Wright (2007) argue that this threat of bankruptcy created by the failure to pay interest motivates organisations to become more efficient. The share of equity in the financing structure is reduced by intensive use of debt. Hence, private equity investors are able to control the majority of stock and to lead to a concentration of ownership. This, in turn, enables private equity firms to monitor and control the strategy of the buyout target firm through an active presence on the board of directors. According to Jensen's free cash flow thesis, the need for monitoring management is partially offset by the effective self-monitoring resulting from managerial ownership.

In this context, the implications of the SOA weaken Jensen's hypothesis at least to a certain degree. As discussed in the previous part, the increased independency requirements for board members implemented with the SOA can reduce the influence of private equity companies in target firms. Therefore, the effect that monitoring from outside is substituted by self-monitoring from inside is supposed to be smaller.

5.5   The Validity of the Free Cash Flow Hypothesis

The question of whether the free cash flow hypothesis is valid has been frequently discussed in literature. In order to answer this question, this paper discusses the most recent findings in research. Cotter and Peck (2001) and Burton et al. (2002) find that increased leverage and realignment of incentives have positive effects on the operating performance of leveraged buyout companies. In addition, Smith (1990) and Holthausen and Larcker (1996) provide evidence of reductions in capital requirements after a buyout and studies of Desbrières and Schatt (2002) and Harris et al. (2005) show significant cost reductions and improved margins and efficiency after a buyout. In contrast to that, other studies by Weir et al. (2005) and Renneboog (2007) cannot find support for the free cash flow hypothesis as a driver of public to private buyouts.

Those different findings suggest that governance mechanisms are not the main driver of LBO returns but nevertheless, they seem to have certain impacts. Therefore, it is reasonable to distinguish in more detail between different characteristics of an LBO e.g. the size of the target firm, the exit mode or the duration of the holding period. Nikoskelainen and Wright (2007) reach the conclusion that size is positively related to value increase, that acquisitions during the holding period are one of the main drivers of LBO returns and that there is a difference between the return characteristics of buyouts and buyins. They argue that small LBOs suffer from a higher bankruptcy risk because they are more vulnerable to industry cycles and short-term business disturbances. Additionally, it might be more difficult for smaller companies to exit due to lack of interest from industry buyers or they do not meet the scale required for an IPO.

Finally it has to be concluded that the latest research does not explicitly support Jensen's theory that governance mechanisms solve agency problems associated with free cash flow and increased equity value. Betzer (2006) also argues in his study about European LBO transactions that the predictions derived from free cash flow hypothesis are not supported in all its details. Due to his results, corporate governance mechanisms do not seem to matter with regard to the probability of a company being taken private. The past operating performance, expected future performance and a company's stock price are the driving forces influencing the probability of a company becoming an LBO target. Those findings give rise to ample additional research in the field of governance mechanisms and in particular to the area of the different value drivers in LBO transactions.

6   Conclusion

"Like any other in America, we [KKR] go driving down the streets looking at all the pretty houses. We see a house and we like it, so we pay the owner a premium price. Like every other American, we borrow money to do it. The average American puts down maybe 10 to 20% to buy a house – a highly leveraged transaction. We do the same thing. So now we own this house [...] we sell the garage. And yet somehow, after a number of years, we sell this house for a compound rate of return of 40% to the next guy." (KKR Partner M. Tokarz, in Baker & Smith (2006), p. 91).

Michael Tokarz's house analogy represents the exact opposite of the Heuschrecken-dispraise. His statement is equally dangerous as it neglects complexity, risks and generalises LBO transactions. The aim of this paper is to provide a true and fair view on LBO transactions, the risks involved and regulatory measurements.

Referring back to the "house analogy", it describes the overall idea of an LBO. However, the paper demonstrates that even though each buyout follows the same sequence of actions, every parameter must be assessed. Target, deal structure, and exist must fit to the deal's respective financial structure. Practice shows that each component entails further implications on the success of a transaction. Therefore, an LBO's complexity cannot be compared to the leveraged acquisition of a house.

Additionally, the analogy employed by Michael Tokarz totally disregards the risks involved. Although, the paper empirically disproves the most frequently used points of critique in the Heuschrecken-debate, it shows that an LBO transaction entails more severe risks than the acquisition of a house. Those risks are the risk of over-gearing and the risk to global debt capital markets. In terms of the former, rising interest rates, decreasing cash flows and the greed of equity investors represent the levers whereas in terms of the latter, event risk is the major factor. Both risks give rise to the discussion about regulatory measurements and governance implications in leveraged buyouts.

The discussion of recent developments in both the American and German corporate governance system showed the existing trade-off between investor orientation and creditor protection. Especially in Germany, legislature must decide how increasing investor orientation can be combined with the necessary creditor protection. Concerning the latter, both, the balance sheet capital based maintenance rule and the Anglo-Saxon solvency test represent appropriate measures in practice. According to the latest findings, however, the balance sheet capital based maintenance rule provides superior protection to creditors.

To conclude, the worst case scenario which has been drawn at the beginning is, unlikely to become reality. Nevertheless, the paper demonstrates that both endogenous parameters, such as high leverage, and exogenous factors, namely interest rates and the economic situation, have a significant influence on the success of an LBO. Since leveraged buyouts represent a significant share of today's M&A activity, its consequences – whether success or failure – will certainly impact the world economy.

References

Achleiter, A. K. & Fingerle, C. H. (2003). Unternehmenswertsteigerung durch Management Buyout. *Working Paper Series,* 01-03.

Adecco: Bilanzprobleme (13.01.2004). *Hamburger Abendblatt.* Retrieved October 20, 2007 from http://www.abendblatt.de/daten/2004/01/13/250635.html

Akin Gump Strauss Hauser & Feld LLP [Akin Gump] (2003). *Sarbanes-Oxley and revised listing standards. Implications for private equity funds (update).* Retrieved October 20, 2007 from http://library.findlaw.com/2003/Mar/31/ 132706.pdf

Anders, G. (1992). *The Barbarians in the Boardroom.* Cambridge: Harvard University Press.

Baker, G. P. & Montgomery, C. A. (1994). Conglomerats and LBO associations. A comparison of organizational forms. *Harvard Business School Working Paper, November 4,* 1-34.

Baker, G. P. & Wruck, K. H. (1989). Organizational Change and Value Creation in Leveraged Buyouts. *Journal of Financial Economics, 25,* 163-190.

Baker, J. P. & Smith, J. D. (2006). *The New Financial Capitalist: Kohlberg Kravis Roberts and the Creation of Corporate Value.* New York: Cambridge University Press.

Betzer, A. (2006). Does Jensen's Free Cash Flow Hypothesis explain European LBOs today? *University of Bonn Working Paper, March 2006,* 1-17.

Bessis, J. (1998). *Risk Management in Banking.* Chichester: Wiley and Sons.

Biggs, B. (2006). *Hedgehogging.* London: Wiley.

Bodie, Z., Kane, A. & Marcus, A. J. (2005). *Investments.* New York: McGraw-Hill.

Bottazzi, L. & Da Rin, M. (2002). Venture Capital in Europe and the Financing of Innovative Companies. *Economic Policy Journal, April 2002,* 231-269.

Brealey, R. A. & Myers, S. C. (2005). *Principles of Corporate Finance.* New York: McGraw-Hill.

Bruner, R. F. (2005). *Deals from Hell.* New Jersey: Wiley and Sons.

Bull, I. (1989). *Management Performance in Leveraged Buyouts: An Empirical Analysis in Leveraged Managements Buyouts, Causes and Consequences.* Illinois: Homewood.

Bumiller, E. (2002). Bush Signs Bill Aimed at Fraud in Corporations. *The New York Times, July 31, 2002*, page A1.

Bundesgesetzblatt (1998). *Teil I Nr. 22 vom 23. April 1998.* Bonn. [Elektronic version].

Bundesgesetzblatt (1998). *Teil I Nr. 24 vom 30. April 1998.* Bonn. [Elektronic version].

Bundesgesetzblatt (2004). *Teil I Nr. 65 vom 4. Dezember 2004.* Bonn [Electronic version]

Bundesgesetzblatt (2004). *Teil I Nr. 69 vom 20. Dezember 2004.* Bonn [Electronic version]

Burton, G. D., Keels, J.K. & Scifres, E. L. (2002). Corporate Restructuring and Performance. An Agency Perspective on the complete Buyout Circle. *Journal of Business Research, 55,* 709-724.

Cotter, J. F. & Peck, S. W. (2001). The Structure of Debt and active Equity Investors. The Case of the Buyout Specialist. *Journal of Financial Economics, 59,* 101-147.

Cumming D. J. & Macintosh, J. G. (2003a). A Cross-Country Comparison of Full and Partial Exits. *Journal of Banking and Finance, 27,* 511-548.

Cumming, D. J. & Macintosh, J.G. (2003b). *Venture Capital Exits in Canada and the United States*, Toronto: University Press

Damodaran, A. (2003). *Investment Philosophies: Successful Investment Philosophies and the Greatest Investors Who Made Them Work.* New York: Wiley and Sons.

Die Zeit (17.04.2005). *Weckrufe für die Stammwähler. SPD-Parteichef Franz Müntefering geißelt Kapital.* Retrieved October 20, 2007 from http://www.zeit.de/2005/16/kapitalkritik?page=all

DeAngelo, H., DeAngelo, L. & Rice, E. (1984). Going Private. Minority Freezeouts and Stockholder Wealth. *Journal of Law and Economics, October 1984,* 367-401.

Desbrières, P. & Schatt, A. (2002). The Impacts of LBOs on the Performance of Acquired Firms. The French Case. *Journal of Business Finance and Accounting, 29,* 695-729.

Dörner, D. & Orth, C. (2003). Bedeutung der Corporate Governance für Unternehmen und Kapitalmärkte. In Pfitzer, N. & Oser, P. (Eds.). *Deutscher Corporate Governance Kodex. Ein Handbuch für Entscheidungsträger.* Stuttgart: Schäffer-Poeschel Verlag.

Durand, H. (2007). Corporate Bond Investors demand Puts for LBO Risk. *Euroweek, 1001*, 107.

Easterwood, J., Seth, A. & Singer, R. (1989). The Impact of Leveraged Buyouts on Strategic Direction. *California Management Review, 32*, 30-43.

Forst, M. (1993). *Struktur und Stabliltät eines Leveraged Management Buy-Out.* Düsseldorf: Unknown Publishers.

Frentz, C. (25.09.2003). *Chronik einer Rekord-Pleite.* Retrieved October 20, 2007 from http://www.manager-magazin.de/unternehmen/artikel/0,2828,178836,00.html

Giot, P. & Schwienbach, A. (2003). *IPO`s, Trade Sale and Liquidations: Modelling Venture Capital Exits using Survival Analysis.* Amsterdam: University Press.

Gompers, P. & Learner, J. (1998). Venture Capital Distributions: Short-Run and Long-Run Reactions. *Journal of Finance, LIII, No. 6*, 2161-2183.

Gompers, P. & Lerner, J. (1999). *The Venture Capital Cycle.* Cambridge: MIT Press.

Graebner, U. A. C. (1991). *Die Auseinandersetzung um Leveraged Buyouts.* Frankfurt am Main: Fritz Knapp Verlag.

Gröne, T. (2005). *Private Equity in Germany: Evaluation of the Value Creation Potential for German Mid-Cap Companies.* Stuttgart: Ibidem Verlag.

Harris, R., Siegel, D. & Wright, M. (2005). Assessing the Impact of management Buyouts on Economic Efficiency. Plant-level Evidence from the United Kingdom. *Review of Economics and Statistics, 87*, 148-153.

Holthausen, R. W. & Larcker, D. F. (1996). The Financial Performance of Reverse Leverage Buyouts. *Journal of Financial Economics, 42*, 293-332.

iTraxx (2007). *iTraxx Europe CDS Indices – Serious Aid.* Retrieved November 7, 2007 from http://www.indexco.com/download/products/cds/itraxx_europe_s8_presentation.pdf

Jensen, M. C. (1986). Agency Costs of Free Cash Flow, Corporate Finance, and Takeovers. *American Economic Review, 76*, 323-329.

Jensen, M. C. & Murphy, K. (1990). CEO Incentives. It's not how much you pay, but how. *Harvard Business Review, 1990*, 138-147.

Kaplan, S. N. (1989). The Effects of Management Buyouts on Operating Performance and Value. *Journal of Financial Economics, 24*, 217-254.

Kaplan, S. N. & Stein, J. C. (1993). The Evolution of Buyout Pricing and Financial Structure in the 1980s. *The Quarterly Journal of Economics, 108*, 313-357.

Kessel, A. (1995). *The Leveraged Buyout in den USA und der Bundesrepublik Deutschland: Eine Agency Theorertische Betrachtungsweise*. Frankfurt am Main: Peter Lang Europäischer Verlag der Wissenschaften.

Kessel, B. (1991). *Management Buy-Out*. Frankfurt am Main: Peter Lang Europäischer Verlag der Wissenschaften.

Kester, W. C. & Luehrman, T. A. (1995). *Rehabilitating the Leveraged Buyout*. Cambridge: Harvard University Press.

Kohlberg Kravis Roberts & Co. (Eds.) (1989). *Presentation on Leveraged Buyouts*. New York: Kohlberg Kravis Roberts.

Köhn, R. (2005). *Der Fall Grohe liefert Zündstoff*. Retrieved November 7, 2007 from http://www.faz.net/s/RubBF53424976DC438985BBA461C86C95A7/Doc~E7E 10CCD32B6E474384C9498425C667D2~ATpl~Ecommon~Scontent.html

Kühn, C. (2006). Capital *Structure Decisions in Institutional Buyouts*. Aachen: Deutscher Universitätsverlag.

Kushner, M. (2004). Searching for exits in a challenging market. *International Financial Law Review*, 95-98.

Lerner, J. & Hardymon, F. (2002). *Venture Capital and Private Equity – A Casebook*. New York: Wiley and Sons.

Loos, N. (2006). *Value Creation in Leveraged Buyouts. Analysis of Factor Driving Private Equity Investment Performance*. St.Gallen: Deutscher Universitäts-Verlag.

Lichtenberg, F. & Siegel, D. (1990). The Effects on Productivity and Related Aspects of Firm Behaviour. *Journal of Financial Economics, 27*, pp. 165–194.

Lieber, D. (2004). Proactive Portfolio Management: Manage now to Realize Returns Later. *The Journal of Private Equity, 1*, 72-82.

Machiraju, H. R. (2003). *Mergers, Acquisitions and Takeovers*. New Delhi: New Age International.

Maier, A. (2006). *Experten erwarten hohe Kreditausfälle*. Retrieved October 20, 2007 from http://www.ftd.de/unternehmen/finanzdienstleister/113392.html

Markey, E. J. (1989). Legislative Views on Management Buyouts. In Amihud, Y. (Ed.). (1989). *Leveraged Management Buyouts: Causes and Consequences*. Homewood: New Century.

Meier, D. (2006). *Post-Investment Value Additions to Buyouts: Analysis of European Private Equity Firms*. Aachen: Deutscher Universitäts-Verlag.

Michel, A. & Sharked, I. (1988). *The Complete Guide to a Successful Leveraged Buyout*. Illinois: Business One Irvin.

Morgan, J. (2006). BoE Highlights Risk of LBO. *Risk, 19*, 11.

Menzies, C. (Ed.). (2004). *Sarbanes-Oxley Act. Professionelles Management interner Kontrollen*. Stuttgart: Schäffer-Poeschel Verlag.

Muscarella, C. J. & Vetsuypens, M. R. (1990). Efficieny and Organizational Structure: A Study of Reverse LBOs. *Journal of Finance, 45*, 1389-1413.

Neff, C. (2003). *Corporate Finance, Innovation, and Strategic Competition*. Berlin: Springer Verlagsgruppe.

Nikoskelainen, E. & Wright, M. (2007). The Impact of Corporate Governance Mechanisms on Value increase in leveraged buyouts. *Journal of Corporate Finance, 13*, 511-537.

Paprottka, S. (1996). *Unternehmenszusammenschlüsse*. Wiesbaden: Gabler Verlag.

Paulson, E. (1999). *The Complete Idiot's Guide to Buying and Selling a Business*. New York: Alpha.

Pellens, B., Fülbier, R. U. & Gassen, J. (2004). *Internationale Rechnungslegung* (5. ed.). Stuttgart: Schäffer-Poeschel Verlag.

Phan, P. H. & Hill, C. W. L. (1995). Organizational Restructuring and Economic Performance in Leveraged Buyouts. *Academy of Management Journal, 38*, 704-706.

Picot, G. (2005). *Handbuch Mergers and Acquisitions: Planung, Durchführung, Integration*. Stuttgart: Schäffer-Poeschel Verlag.

Pohlhausen, T. E. (2003). *Technology Buyouts: Technology Buyouts: Valuation, Market Screening Application, Opportunities in Europe*. Aachen: Deutscher Universitäts-Verlag.

Povaly, S. (2007). *Private Equity Exits: Divestment Process Management for Leveraged Buyouts*. Berlin: Springer Verlagsgruppe.

PricewaterhouseCoopers [PwC] & Bundesverband der Deutschen Industrie e.V. [BDI] (2005). *Corporate Governance in Deutschland. Entwicklungen und Trends vor internationalem Hintergrund*. Retrieved October 20, 2007 from http://www.bdi-online.de/Dokumente/Recht-Wettbewerb-Versicherungen/BDI_PwC_Studie.pdf

Renneboog, L., Simons, T. & Wright, M. (2007). Why do Firms go Private in the UK? *Journal of Corporate Finance, 13*, 591-628.

Ross, S. A., Westerfield, R. W. & Jaffe, J. (2005). *Corporate Finance* (7. ed.). New York: McGraw-Hill Irwin.

Sachverständigenrat zur Begutachtung der gesamtwirtschaftlichen Lage (2005). *Jahresgutachten 2005/06. Die Chancen nutzen. Reformen mutig voranbringen.* Retrieved October 20, 2007 from http://www.sachverstaendigenrat-wirtschaft.de/gutacht/ga-content.php?gaid=45&node=f

Sappington, D. (1983). Limited Liability Contracts between Principal and Agent. *Journal of Economic Theory, 1983,* 1-21.

Securities and Exchange Commission [SEC] (2007). *The Investor's Advocate. How the SEC Protects Investors, Maintains Market Integrity, and Facilitates Capital Formation.* Retrieved October 20, 2007 from http://www.sec.gov/about/whatwedo.shtml#create

Sheahan, M. (2007). Troubled LBO Debt Pipeline Still Awaits First Data Sale. *High Yield Report, 18, No. 35,* 1-8.

Shleifer, A. & Vishny, R. (1986). Large Shareholders and Corporate Control. *Journal of Political Economics, June 1986,* 461-488.

Skousen, K. F. (1991). *An Introduction to the SEC* (5. ed.). Cincinnati: South Western College Publishing.

Smith, A. J. (1990). Corporate Ownership Structure and Performance. The Case of Management Buyouts. *Journal of Financial Economics, 27,* 143-164.

Tanski, J. (2002). WorldCom. Eine Erläuterung zu Rechnungslegung und Corporate Governance. *DStR, 46,* 2003.

Unknown (2006). Citigroup Hoists Up Sails to Protect against LBO Risk. *Euroweek, 983,* 12.

Unknown (2006). The Stand-Off Begins. *Euromoney, 37,* 12-14.

Unknown (n.a.). *Finanzielle Risiken durch Leveraged Buyouts und die Gläubigerschutzwirkung alternativer Kapitalerhaltungskonzepte.* Unpublished Paper in a Review Process, 1-38.

Warner, D. & Ceberio, E. (2004). The new Corporate Governance Requirements. Why Private Equity Sponsors should care. *Weil, Gotshal & Manges LLP Private Equity Alert, January 2004,* 1-6.

Weir, C., Laing, D. & Wright, M. (2005) Incentive Effects, Monitoring Mechanisms and the Market for Corporate Control. An Analysis of the Factors affecting

Public to Private Transactions in the UK. *Journal of Business Finance and Accounting, 32,* 909-944.

Whitehouse, M. (2005). LBOs May Spoil the Corporate-Bond Party. *Wall Street Journal, Eastern Edition, 246,* C1-C4.

Wright, M., Robbie, K., Thomson, S. & Starkey, K. (1993). Longlivety and the Life Cycle of Management Buy-Outs. *Strategic Management Journal, 15,* 215-227.